The Rebirth of the American Dream

"How Abolishing our Current Tax Code and the IRS will lead to the Next Huge Economic Growth Boom!"

Don Allen Holbrook

Copyright © 2013 Don Allen Holbrook

All rights reserved.

ISBN:1494395592
ISBN-13:9781494395599

DEDICATION

This book is dedicated to all of us as Americans. We have taken the greatest economic pounding the global economy can dish out and we are still standing. But the abuse of power and economic harm done to all of us is not necessary and in fact it is not what our founding fathers envisioned for us. If we want the simple standard they set for us of the pursuit of life, liberty and happiness we have to regain control of our national fiscal situation and kick start economic growth. Nearly ninety percent of Americans have suffered these past five years and our suffering will continue if we do not reboot, rebuild and restore the true economic foundation of the spirit of America. This will take all of us to be part of the solution and advocate for change. The restoration of the American Dream can be directly linked to economic prosperity for all citizens without sacrificing the ideals that have made us America and moving towards something less than true capitalism. This book is for all of you ready and willing to engage in grassroots efforts to advocate for positive economic change and hold our elected officials responsible to serve our needs not special interests groups.

CONTENTS

	Acknowledgments	i
1	Why do We Need to Act Now?	Pg 1
2	History of United States Taxation	Pg 5
3	The Scandalous Behavior of the IRS	Pg 12
4	The FairTax Proposition Explained	Pg 18
5	Flat Tax versus a FairTax Comparison	Pg 30
6	High Taxes Hurt our Economy	Pg 41
7	Failed Efforts of the Past	Pg 45
8	The IRS must be Minimized to a Regulatory Role	Pg 50
9	What would the New Tax Code Be?	Pg 59
10	Final Thoughts	Pg 71

ACKNOWLEDGMENTS

Thank you to all my friends and family members that have tolerated my rants and tirades about how our country is not getting better but actually slipping away from our true American ideals. Without your encouragement I would not have the patience and persistence to continue to write and advocate for the changes that most American's believe are necessary to get our nation back on track. I especially want to thank my Mom & Dad for supporting and believing in me all these years. I want to thank my wife Laurie for putting up with me through all my ups and downs and for giving me our two precious sons. I love all of you…

CHAPTER ONE

Why Do We Need To Act Now?

The IRS's bad year just keeps getting worse. The fact remains that under the Obama administration the IRS has gotten FAR TOO Egregious towards those American's hurt by the Global Financial Crisis of 2008-2012. This five year meltdown affected ninety eight percent (98%) of American's in a very bad way... most losing ground on their real estate equity, disposable incomes shrinkage, job security vaporized and savings and retirement exhausted in futile attempts to stay afloat. The record number of bankruptcies should attest to that alone. Only the very top 2% of American's had the cash to not only stay or adjust to the economic crisis but also purchase for pennies the losses of their fellow American's for their own profits. Let's not forget that much of this was allowed and funded by their cozy banking and financial relationships with the federal elixir called TARP (Toxic Asset Relief Program). Politicians, Corporations and the Media have become far too cozy of friends in the past two decades and the loss of accountability to us as taxpayers has been astronomical. The triad has worse yet aligned to sell us their propaganda so that we begin to believe there is truly no better way. This has begun to erode and destroy the very spirit of the average American. If you have such conversations with friends and neighbors you can see the loss of trust, hope and belief in our core values in their eyes and hear it in their voices.

Now those of us hurt by the enormous losses to the rest of our country and our need to find work and funds in many cases forced us into self-employment, where paying taxes or eating was our most difficult choice. You know most American's chose to eat and provide shelter for their families.

Fast forward to 2012-2013... many American's are just beginning to get back on their feet and now the IRS is attacking them and not only demanding those back taxes, which they can't afford to pay, but not being willing to even negotiate on a fair payment catch up plan. Then to top all of this off now Obama is putting them in charge of the mandatory health insurance and giving them additional free reign to terrorize the American taxpayer for yet more money for the government and less disposable income for the working stiffs...normal trying to recover hard working Americans.

Currently the Local, State and Federal government consumes approximately 9.9% for state and local taxes, 15% for Social Security and Medicare, and up to 28% for income, so it can mean as high as 52% of someone's cash in various forms of taxes and fees. This does not include licensure, gasoline, utilities, telecommunications, and other forms of taxes. (1) Even this is not enough for our rock star politicians who live nothing like those they get elected by... well with the exception of their major corporate donors.

This over aggressive and wasteful tax and fiscal policy of the United States has to be toppled and replaced with something that can provide for all American's the items we desire most and allow us to keep more of our cash than we give to the government. Something is just wrong when our government gets more of our earned money then we do! This should sound so much like the time of the Middle Ages when kings and queens extracted such heavy taxes that we eventually overthrew them for the creation of governments. Now that self-created machine of fairness has become a green eyed monster that must be put down for our own good.

Don Allen Holbrook

CHAPTER TWO

History of United States Taxation

Let's take a quick look at Taxation History in the United States. From the 1790's until the eve of World War I, the US relied mostly on Tariffs for its' central government revenue. Tariffs are taxes on imports to our country. Then in 1913 newly elected Woodrow Wilson called for the creation of a modest income tax of approximately 7% on our wages, 1% on the net personal wages and a surtax of 6% on all incomes above $500,000. This was the ratification of the 16th Amendment to the constitution. It marked the creation of the most onerous agency in the United States government the Internal Revenue Service.

The United States had some minor experience with an income tax prior to the 16th amendment. In order to help

pay for the war effort in the American Civil War, Congress imposed its first personal income tax in 1861. It was part of the Revenue Act of 1861 (3% of all incomes over US $800; rescinded in 1872). Congress also enacted the Revenue Act of 1862, which levied a 3% tax on incomes above $600, rising to 5% for incomes above $10,000. So this first tax was also a progressive tax. The likely revisions to the minimum income tax levels of taxation were to capture more revenue for the central governments use (sound familiar). Rates were raised in 1864 yet again, as our earlier politicians already began to show their ability to abuse a powerful tool such as this. This income tax was repealed in 1872. The American people did not like the concept of being taxed on their toils, it probably felt too much like the old colonial days of being taxed by an unseen, unresponsive and unaccountable monarch. We finally put an end to that with our revolutionary war. In those days the Monarch of England imposed many forms of excise taxes but the most notable was the Stamp Tax (which required that all documents, papers of enterprise and of any legal standing had to carry a stamp, which was a fee or tax paid to the crown.) Today this stamp act would be more akin to a modern proposal being brought back into use from these colonial days, it is called a transaction tax. We are already seeing those in Europe and other places. This creates a small fee for every commerce transaction. It is a sliver almost unnoticeable until you add all the tens of millions up per day and then it amounts to an enormous amount of money.

Prior to the Great Depression, which began officially in 1929, the following economic problems were considered great hazards to the working-class in American:

- The U.S. had no federal-government-mandated retirement savings; consequently, for many workers (those who could not afford both to save for retirement and to pay for living expenses), the end of their work careers was the end of all income and they fell in to twilight of poverty.
- Similarly, the U.S. had no federal-government-mandated disability income insurance to provide for citizens disabled by injuries (of any kind—work-related or non-work-related); consequently, for most people, a disabling injury meant no more income if they had not saved enough money to prepare for such an event (since most people have little to no income except

earned income from work). So if you became disabled you were financially ruined.

- In addition, there was no federal-government-mandated disability income insurance to provide for people unable to ever work during their lives, such as anyone born with severe mental retardation. This made the care of such folks either inhumane or an enormous burden on their family, which most families had little ability to properly afford to care for such instances and feed their other family members.

- Finally, the U.S. had no federal-government-mandated health insurance for the elderly; consequently, for many workers (those who could not afford both to save for retirement and to pay for living expenses), the end of their work careers was the end of their ability to pay for medical care. This of course meant that most folks died of very curable diseases due to lack of proper healthcare affordability.

Congress Responds with an Entire New Set of Central Government Initiatives that have spawned the Great Society as it was dubbed.

In the 1930s, the New Deal introduced Social Security to rectify the first three problems (retirement, injury-induced disability, or congenital disability). It introduced the FICA tax as the means to pay for Social Security. The 1940's saw the introduction of payroll taxes to further cover these issues.

In the 1960s, Medicare was introduced to rectify the fourth problem (health care for the elderly). The FICA tax was increased in order to pay for this expense.

Gift or Inheritance Taxes- Double taxation is the real issue.

In the 1880s and 1890s many states passed inheritance taxes, which taxed the inheritors on the receipt of their inheritance. While many objected to the application of an inheritance tax, some including Andrew Carnegie and John D. Rockefeller supported increases in the taxation of inheritance. They were very civically minded at their core, but they could realize that this meant that the majority of folks would be subjected to this tax not just the rich of each era.

At the beginning of the 20th century President Theodore Roosevelt advocated the application of a progressive inheritance tax on the federal level.

In 1916, Congress adopted the present federal estate tax, which instead of taxing the wealth that an inheritor inherited as occurred in the state inheritance taxes it taxed the wealth of a donor's estate upon transfer.

Later, Congress passed the Revenue Act of 1924, which imposed the gift tax, a tax on gifts given by the donor at the federal level.

Today we have a whole host of taxes that still are not enough to sufficiently pay for the cost of operating our government and their proposals as of publishing of this book are to either raise more taxes (not cut costs) or increase more fees (still taxes).

CHAPTER THREE

The Scandalous Behavior of the IRS

The starting point has to be the most heinous agency in our government the IRS. Let's just look at their record recently;

They were caught red handed in scandals targeting political groups that opposed the administration and also for leaking thousands of taxpayer social security numbers ... the holy grail of Identity fraud hucksters and hackers... That's why you need to operate on the assumption that your personal data is going to be leaked at some point if this is any indication of IRS data privacy we are all in trouble.

Now to top all that off, the IRS couldn't just sit back and watch the banks have all the fun so they got themselves into the banking business, figuring wow the banks really have a great racket going... more than one million taxpayers took advantage of this program. Now the IRS has withheld their tax refunds for over 4 months due to pure confusion and misdirection of applied payments.

Something I am recently fully aware of. I send them payments and they lose them and claim they have not received them. How convenient for them putting all the proof on us and no responsibility for such screw-ups such as their own.

All the taxpayers involved in the glitch took advantage of a one-time, misnamed First Time Homebuyer tax "credit" offered during the 2008 tax year, a program that turned out to be a one again failed effort by Congress to prop up the then-imploding housing market and fatten up the bankers. Homebuyers who took advantage didn't actually receive a credit — they were granted what was essentially an interest-free loan of up to $7,500, to be paid back in $500 increments starting in 2010. Imagine your disdain when you are told that your grant is really a loan with the one agency that has the worst reputation for being fair with people on the planet and with such power they can confiscate your assets, income and other things if you don't pay it on their schedule. Now Congress did go ahead and fix this in the Subsequent versions of the program, which then granted homebuyers an outright tax credit, so the 2008 users already have something to moan about and no recourse. Why? Because it was the law is their basis for harming us.

IRS systems weren't set up to handle the many variables that ultimately came from the program. WHAT, you mean they didn't think this through? Of course not! Why because the IRS has no accountability for responsibility such as how to calculate repayment of the loans if buyers get divorced, or end up in foreclosure. Another particularly troublesome and unexpected problem is that many taxpayers are paying more than the minimum $500 annual payment in an effort to pay off the loan early. But the IRS is unclear as to whether that is allowable... come on, just laughable.

Here is another great use of our funds... the IRS pays a former Swiss Banker $104 million reward for blowing the whistle on thousands of tax payers that have such Swiss Accounts.

But the IRS whistle blower was also guilty of the very actions he was turning states evidence on... he pleaded guilty in 2007 to the tax fraud, then served four years but upon his release applied for his $104 million reward... not bad $26 Million per year to a convicted convict in the financial industry.

"IRS Is an Agency in Crisis"

Hey the IRS employees have figured out that not only should they live like their elected bosses in Congress because they to are entitled to it but they need employee junkets too! Internal Revenue Service is in a boatload of trouble already for their lack of accountability, a congressional committee charged with rooting out corruption in government is now investigating the tax agency for blowing tens of millions of dollars on employee conferences.

The probe comes on the heels of the scandal for the ages, in which the IRS targeted conservative groups applying for tax-exempt status. Organizations with conservative-sounding phrases such as patriot and Tea Party in their titles were singled out by the agency, according to a **Treasury Inspector General report** that ignited outrage among both Democrats and Republicans alike. Though illegal, this witch-hunt against conservatives was rampant at the highest levels of the agency, according to the Treasury watchdog. A truly modern day Watergate but this time it is the wolves in the chicken coop running the chicken farm for their own greed and malicious leverage.

This week's IRS scandal du jour involves $50 million that the beleaguered agency spent on hundreds of conferences for its employees between 2010 and 2012.

The conference spending includes $4 million for a 2010 gathering in southern California in which IRS employees stayed in lavish presidential suites that cost American taxpayers $1,500 to $3,500 per night. Attendees also got free alcohol and tickets to see the area's professional baseball team. To inspire IRS staff, more than a dozen speakers were paid $135,000 in fees, including one who got a whopping $17,000 to talk about "leadership through art."

Just a few years ago the IRS came under fire for allowing 1 million foreigners—many in the U.S. illegally— who were allowed to **improperly claim close to $9 billion in tax credits even though they did not provide** valid Social Security numbers on their return. Not long after that, the tax agency got in trouble for handing out $33 million in bogus electric car credits. They are the most inept at handling money I have ever witnessed other than Congress itself.

The report by the Treasury Inspector General for Tax Administration, which was obtained by ***The Washington Post*** in advance of its release, criticizes the IRS for lax oversight of foreigners who use an alternative form of **identification instead of a Social Security number.** Many of the foreigners who use the code, known as an Individual Taxpayer Identification Number, **are illegal immigrants, according to government officials and immigration experts.** In a statement, IRS inspector general J. Russell George, who wrote the report released on Tuesday, called it **'disturbing' that more than $11 billion in improper payments were being handed out each year.**

CHAPTER FOUR

The Fair Tax Proposition Explained

On the surface, conservatives and progressives seem to be in agreement about what should be done about the IRS scandals, they need to be completely shut down or overhauled and reigned in from their terror tactics and misuse of power:

However, abuse of IRS power has been going on for almost 80 years. It began under FDR, not long after the IRS was created and empowered by President Woodrow Wilson (Democrat). Today the reality is beginning to sink in to most Americans; there is only one way to ensure that something like this never happens again. The IRS must be abolished, the 16th Amendment must be repealed, and a new form of a FairTax must replace most existing federal taxes, which most likely would be a national retail sales tax.

Certainly, what transpired at the IRS in the years after it's creation would not have surprised James Madison.

The IRS is one of the two great Central Government instruments of progressivism (the other is the Federal Reserve). Progressivism holds that, when our founding fathers wrote the U.S. Constitution, James Madison and the other Founders basically got it wrong. Control over the lives of ordinary Americans should not be vested in the people themselves, but should instead be wielded by experts in Washington. Those experts know what is best for us and giving us such choices would be dangerous to our own well being... Oh Come On! Because Madison's Constitution does not provide for this kind of government, the Constitution must be "progressively" dismantled and/or ignored for this to be tolerated.

It is not surprising that our progressive President, who published an "enemies list" on his campaign website, now claims that he had nothing to do with the subsequent IRS harassment of people on his list. Progressivism is totalitarian in impulse. It is an ideology where the ends justify the means. It sounds more like a mad ruler from the medieval ages to me.

To progressives, it makes perfect sense to use the powers of government to promote election victories for progressive candidates. The most fundamental belief of progressivism is that, we act in order for the highest good, "for their own good," control over every aspect of people's lives must be transferred to unelected, unaccountable "experts," such as of course the IRS. Nothing must be allowed to get in the way of this because they know what is best for us all in the end.

The Founders saw the dangers in direct taxation, and that's why they prohibited it when they wrote the Constitution. The latest IRS scandal should be a major wakeup call to all Americans. The 16th Amendment was a mistake then and is an enormous FUBAR today. The income tax gives the federal government more information about us than they need, and direct power over, citizens than is compatible with freedom as our nations' founding fathers wanted for us all. The only permanent solution to the problem of IRS abuse is to abolish the IRS and institute a more FairTax policy.

The FairTax is a simple national retail sales tax. Administering it would not involve collecting any information regarding individual citizens and thus there would be no need even for illegals to avoid paying their fair share. The FairTax would be easily capable of collecting sufficient revenue to replace our current individual and corporate income taxes, payroll taxes, and death taxes. We could track the taxes paid by taxpayer IDs for those wanting to use their vouchers for a portion of their workforce benefits such as retirement, disability, healthcare and unemployment. Yes it would discriminate against providing such benefits to those here in our country ILLEGALLY... but that is fair. You want your benefits you have to be registered and LEGALLY in our country. What it would do is also make sure that everyone including visitors' pay for the use of our national services. I LIKE THAT don't you?

The benefits of a more FairTax go far beyond restoring and safeguarding our liberty. Some economic experts have estimated the FairTax that it would also produce a rapid, perhaps robust, expansion of real GDP (RGDP) and employment gains.

The current FairTax plan proposal before Congress also includes a "Prebate" feature, under which every American individual (or family) would receive a monthly check equal to the FairTax that they would pay if they earned an income at the poverty line and spent all of it on items subject to the FairTax. Right now, the Prebate would amount to $335.38/month for a family of four. This negates the harmful impact on those folks just getting by financially, of course yes they do have to be LEGAL citizens of the United States.

The Prebates could be capitalized to provide every American with a line of credit or voucher type system, with no repayment risk to the federal government. This credit line could replace all of the federal "social safety net" programs targeted at working-age adults and their children. It could also provide every American turning 18 with a "grubstake", access to sufficient capital to get a reasonable start in life. It could be utilized for education and other growing expenses that a knowledge and smart economy is in need of today. Our cost of education is also out of control and far too expensive to most working class Americans pocket books.

Because the FairTax would not tax savings and investment at all, and because its compliance costs would be nil, the FairTax would deliver the highest rate of economic growth of any tax system and take away the basis for taxpayers to hide their funds off shore. This would bring capital back to our own shores for reinvestment into job creating opportunities that grow our own local economies.

Under the FairTax, most tax savvy large corporations in the world would move their headquarters to the U.S. to avoid the corporate taxes imposed by other nations. America would become a multinational corporations' preferred platform for export manufacturing. Illegal alien and foreign billionaires and millionaires would be running to our country begging for asylum and citizenship.

A host of economic experts believe that it would not be unreasonable to expect that, with a new FairTax platform in place, the U.S. real GDP (RGDP) would grow at more than 5% per year for a long time.

So, what difference does it make to us as a nation fiscally whether our real economic growth rate over the next 100 years is 2.26% (the CBO's latest forecast) or 4.00% (a conservative growth rate estimate for a FairTax regime) by the Fair Tax economic experts?

A 4.00% RGDP growth rate would increase our cumulative RGDP (in 2012 dollars) over the next 100 years by 239%, from $6.1 quadrillion (thousand trillion) to $20.7 quadrillion. The present value of RGDP over this 100-year period (i.e., the PV100) would increase by 146%, rising to $3.3 quadrillion from $1.3 quadrillion.

At a 4.00% RGDP growth rate, our federal debt would quickly become insignificant. Both Social Security and Medicare would be sustainable with no benefit-cutting "reforms" but that does not mean we should continue with this program without healthcare voucher and retirement voucher institution of individual choice for our workers. I favor the choice option rather than a continued wage tax at all.

With 4.00% RGDP growth, a FairTax rate of 10.8% inclusive (12.2% add-on) would give the federal government the same spending power over the next 100 years as would our current tax system coupled with the CBO's 2.26% RGDP growth rate. That is, the PV100 of federal revenues would be $234 trillion in both cases. (In the FairTax case, the $234 trillion would be net of the Prebates paid out.)

Right now, the federal debt held by the public plus the unfunded liabilities of Social Security and Medicare amount to something less than $100 trillion. A FairTax rate of 13.3% inclusive (15.3% add-on) would yield $334 trillion (PV100) in federal revenues, thus allowing us to both maintain spending at planned levels and also pay off all of our obligations.

A move to the FairTax would benefit the poor and the middle class the most. What "the 99%" need most are more jobs and higher real wages. The only thing that can produce these is fast economic growth.

The FairTax would also reduce income inequality. Capital and labor split the sales dollar, with capital taking its share first. The FairTax will lower the cost of capital, and this will raise the percentage of GDP going to workers.

Even if someone worked in the underground economy and received all of their income in cash, they would not be able to avoid paying the FairTax when they go to purchase goods and services. Obviously, if people who don't report their income are forced to start paying taxes, the citizens who currently report all of their income can pay less. This should be somewhat obvious. Many liberals try to make this look like the FAIR Tax would harm folks, but in the end it benefits almost everyone here legally.

One feature of the FairTax that would especially benefit poor people is that each person's Prebate could be capitalized into a line of credit. Assuming a 13.3% (inclusive) FairTax rate, the federal government could afford to lend each American turning 18 up to $44,130. The government would face no repayment risk in doing so, because the new adult's Prebate would fully service this amount of debt. This could then be targeted for their education or workforce skills and requirements for a new occupation. Arming our future workforce with a great mind and skills is our best competitive economic development strategy to maintain our global leadership in economic prowess.

Upon enactment of the FairTax, the federal government could extend to a family of four (two 30-year-old adults, a 4-year-old, and a 2-year-old) a $100,910 line of credit. Once again, there would be no risk to the government, because the family's Prebates would cover the debt. This can be applied to their homeownership to reduce their debt load. I am of course in favor of making such loans restricted to specific purposes that improve their fiscal responsibility and long-term economic stability. This could be used to pay-off and then eliminate the entire second mortgage industry, which in my opinion got American's far too far in debt and allowed them and then the world to be exploited financially.

The current scandal demonstrates that the IRS cannot be "reformed" into something compatible with a free society they are oriented towards being government endorsed financial thugs. It is a creation of progressivism, and, at its core, progressivism holds that individual freedom is obsolete then so is our Republic and our core values, I think not.

Why The Fair TAX WOULD WORK!

The current federal income tax system is clearly broken -- unfair, overly complex, and almost impossible for most Americans to understand. But there is a reasonable, nonpartisan alternative that is both fair and easy to understand. A system that allows you to keep your whole paycheck and only pay taxes on what you spend.

The FairTax is a national sales tax that treats every person equally and allows American businesses to thrive, while generating the same tax revenue as the current four-million-word-plus IRS tax code. Under the FairTax, every person living in the United States pays a sales tax on purchases of new goods and services, excluding necessities due to the Prebate. The FairTax rate after necessities is 23% and equal to the lowest current income tax bracket (15%) combined with employee payroll taxes (7.65%), both of which will be eliminated.

Curious? Let's look at what their organization promoting says it would do for most Americans.

Americans Would Keep Their Entire Paycheck

For the first time in recent history, American workers will get to keep every dime they earn. By eliminating federal income taxes and payroll taxes, your salary or hourly wage is exactly what you'll deposit in the bank. This of course would have to include voting that states cannot tax income as well as cities making it clearly a federal constitutional reform.

Social Security & Medicare Funding

Benefits will not change. The FairTax actually proposes to put these programs on a more solid funding foundation. Instead of being funded by taxes on workers' wages, which is a small pool, they'll be funded by taxes on overall consumption by **all** residents and visitors alike. This would be made truly effective if we included a complete workforce benefits reform by constitutional mandate that all workers receive a voucher for their retirement investments, healthcare, disability insurance and unemployment insurance for their own plan selection under a regulated federal set of guidelines by private sector providers.

Get A Tax Refund In Advance On Purchases Of Basic Necessities

The FairTax provides a progressive program called a Prebate. This gives every legal resident household an "advance refund" at the beginning of each month so that purchases made up to the poverty level are tax-free. The Prebate prevents an unfair burden on low-income families. The Prebate also can be targeted for educational costs and homeownership loans if the law provides for such advance loans against your earnings.

Pay Tax On Only What You Spend…Everyone consumes… so everyone will pay his or her fair share!

Be in control of your financial destiny. You alone can control your tax burden. If you're thrifty, you'll pay lower taxes than somebody who is not. Most importantly, you'll be taxed fairly and be capable of deciding what you really want to purchase or not. All levels of society make purchases even those living here illegally. This system would actually capture taxes from those that do not normally participate and thus make our system more fair and realistic to those living here legally.

Everyone Pays Their Fair Share

Tax evasion and the underground economy cost each taxpayer an additional $2,500 every year! But by taxing new products and services consumed, the FairTax puts everyone in the country at the same level at the cash register. Further, only legal residents are eligible for the Prebate so this will eliminate most of the fraudulent tax returns the IRS has sent in the past few years amounting to billions is lost US taxpayer funds. As I said earlier this is a fair and equitable system to make sure that only legal taxpayers benefit from our tax contributions.

The IRS Is No Longer Needed… This should be the Biggest Celebration in our History since our July 4th Declaration of Independence!

No more complicated tax forms, individual audits, or intrusive federal bureaucracy and attack dog oriented bureaucrats that are not accountable or responsible for their actions to anyone. Retailers will collect the FairTax just as they do now with state sales taxes at the point of purchase. All money will be collected and remitted to the U.S. Treasury, and both the retailers and states will be paid a fee for their collection service. Furthermore, every state and city can be included in this system to further eliminate property taxes by increasing local sales taxes to accomplish the feudalism design purposes of their current property tax code driven system. I might remind you that such taxes have been around since Rome and Medieval Dark Ages through today… so there has to be a better way to provide for those services fairly. I believe the consumption tax system is the best route to do so for all the vexing taxes we must be obligated to pay for our cost of governance.

The Rebirth of the American Dream

CHAPTER FIVE

FLAT Tax versus a FAIR TAX Comparison

American public discourse, particularly on the Internet, includes a large portion of our population that is perpetually honked off, offended, irritated and eager to unleash the awesome power of their ALL CAPS digital rage against any idea, no matter how much it may make sense or not. I am not a big fan of blogging as an actual vehicle to effectuate actual change, because there are so many irresponsible and uncivilized and mean spirited bloggers it makes sorting out those with genuine good meaning and solid factual arguments much more time consuming. But as a vehicle to communicate concepts and rally grassroots efforts I do think it can be a powerful weapon for change. This does require that we still follow some civil rules of decorum if some disagree with our views. Nonetheless, the battle for the new tax code will largely be waged via the Internet via emails and bloggers in my opinion.

But for all the hullabaloo around the IRS these past few years, with many denoting the agencies arrogance, overarching increased invasion into our personal affairs, and the overwrought zealous antics of the IRS agents in general, there has not emerged any kind of reasoned argument in favor of keeping the tax authority just the way it is and allowing it to further harm our citizenry.

What has come to the forefront is a healthy debate between two credible, if not complementary, alternatives to America's current egregious and heinous tax system. The debate is should we move to a Fair Tax or a Flat Tax?

Many folks do not clearly understand the difference between the two rival competitors for collecting our taxes in a more acceptable and humane and equitable manner than the current heavy-handed Monarchy of the IRS Agency.

Simply put, would consumption tax on goods and services (Fair Tax), or a single, small rate of tax on income (Flat Tax) is a better way to fund our government? The short answer is that either would be preferable to the Byzantine, corrupt tax system America has now, and most would agree with that. In my book the "Next America-Moving Beyond a Fragile Economy," I discussed the introduction of a hybrid form of taxation. Combining both the Fair Tax concept of a national sales tax with a flat tax on certain items. By doing this we could keep the taxes from being so enormous on any one individual, family and of course business. The debate often overlooks the corporate income tax situation when we discuss the income tax solutions. In order to rid ourselves of the IRS, we must of course have a solution that includes corporations or the IRS monster will remain alive and well. We must give no basis for why the agency should be necessary to exist at all.

Folks are fond of saying you can't replace something with nothing such as our current tax code. This is, of course, complete rubbish, replacing something like our current tax code with nothing new, will only exasperate our national debt. Leaving the current tax code and simply raising taxes won't work either, it would require far too much of our wages to tax our way out simply on income. Creating a more robust and instantaneous tax collection system would go a long way toward solving its monumental debt and deficit problems. Not to say the least of which best results would be to finally behead the IRS green dragon. Most Americans do agree that we do need to pay for our public sector somehow. We need to make progress and it behooves us to consider which of these worthy ideas would work best or perhaps a hybrid model is truly the answer.

First, the Fair Tax: There is legislative support for this approach, as the Fair Tax Act of 2013 works its way through Congress, sponsored by Rep. Rob Woodall of Georgia as H.R.25 in the House, and by Sen. Saxby Chambliss, also of Georgia, as S.122 in the Senate. It is encouraging that this spirit of debate is moving forward.

The gist of the current Fair Tax plan is to phase out the IRS over three years, replacing all personal income taxes with a sales tax on new goods and services, excluding necessities such as groceries and such, of 23 percent. This figure is reached by combining the 15% income tax bracket with 7.65% employee payroll taxes, both of which would be eliminated. As to that last, fairtax.org stresses that its plan eliminates the payroll tax, and this is not an insignificant feature. But the current plan does not create a system whereby citizens can then use the 7.65 portion to direct their own retirement, healthcare, unemployment and disability needs. I firmly believe that the creation of a voucher system would best accomplish this feat. Then the federal government can regulate the requirements for private sector providers to compete for managing our workforce benefits on a self-directed basis. I personally would rather see the national sales tax at about 25% to provide for this form of individual voucher system for our payroll/workforce benefits.

Most working Americans lament their deductions each week as they watch their actual take home pay shrink away, particularly those with lower earnings, they can feel the bite of payroll taxes even more sharply when they get paid, even if they do not end up with a federal income tax liability for the year, they are stressed about the possibility each year. If WE THE PEOPLE mean what we say about simplifying the tax code and really want this to happen, then whatever system we endorse and use needs to be straightforward and clear, and should account for whatever effect, if any, payroll and Social Security, and other workforce benefits that we desire without further taxing take-home wages. What cannot be allowed are the adoption of a national sales tax and the continuation of personal income taxes. I fear that most of all.

A Flat Tax of, perhaps, ten (10%) to fifteen (15%) percent should mean exactly that — not ten (10%) to Fifteen (15%) percent, plus additional levies for retirees, unemployment, etc., that are not normally part of the income tax conversation.

If that can be accomplished, there is much to be said for the simplicity and transparency of a Flat Tax. Sen. Ted Cruz of Texas and The Heritage Foundation are among those calling for this approach. Americans spend billions of hours and hundreds of billions of dollars trying to comply with the country's impossibly complex tax code. The opportunity cost to the productive economy is extraordinary. Now we are also seeing many of our affluent American's give up and renounce their citizenship over the abusive tax code and the high cost of actual taxation in the United States. The renouncing of US citizenship has tripled since 2011.

Something that is often lost in income tax discussions is that these rates also apply to small businesses, which create two-thirds of the new jobs in America, and almost all of which file at individual rates. If a Flat Tax can eliminate the expensive and time-consuming task of tax preparation, not only for individuals but for job-creators as well, that would be a boon to America's beleaguered employment market.

One additional discussion should be the curbing of corporate abuse and excessive write offs by corporations. Contrary to popular belief creating a national gross receipts tax on business corporations would be fair and more equitable than all the other hidden and intrusive attempts the government attempts to use to get money from the private sector. No more inventory taxes, export taxes, etc., instead a flat corporate revenue tax of probably between three (3%) percent to five (5%) percent would be far more efficient. This would also not place the entire burden of paying for our central government on the citizens' pocket books directly.

In addition, if we do not address corporate income we will leave loopholes that could allow the IRS to survive with some basis for an argument for their needed continuation.

As to revenues, economists are all over the board on what to expect from the incorporation of any number of new tax code systems. You will find very intelligent people convinced that a Fair Tax or a Flat Tax couldn't replace the revenue raised by the current system Income Tax; conversely, you will find super smart proponents of these ideas who say we cannot afford not to adopt them if we are to regain real fiscal stability. Whom to believe?

Would either plan get us in the ballpark of where we need to be?

Certainly, they can, and if the political climate that enables either of these policies to be enacted also facilitates spending cuts on what is reasonable from the perspective of the average taxpayer desired use of their funds. The last two presidents, aided by Congresses led by both parties, have each added a more than a trillion dollars each (and counting) to the federal budget over the past dozen years.

Despite this sharp increase in spending, recent silly-grandstanding surrounding the debate of federal budgets reminds us that many insist the current level of government expenditure, no matter how high, is a sacred, necessary, steady state, such that even one penny cut might sure devastation in the future and our loss of economic greatness. Well I would argue that not doing so would absolutely create the exact argument they use for not cutting our expenditures and abolishing our tax code in favor of something that will actually work and be fair and equitable to all citizens. Let's not forget our current code has no resemblance or requirement of being fair and equitable to all of us equally, just those of us that pay taxes and are legally admitting to being here.

As a republic, we can take that risk. So, if a Fair Tax or Flat Tax can get us close enough to the revenue we need, even if it requires pruning the tsarist, rock star and out of touch with their voters' lifestyles of our so-called public servants, so be it. They need to remember public service is supposed to be something of a personal sacrifice not a get rich and be above the law scheme.

Mission creep will also be an issue; with either a Fair Tax or a Flat Tax if history has taught us anything it is that we should not expect our politicians to give up their perks too easily. Lest we forget, when the income tax started in 1913, the top marginal rate was a whopping seven (7%) percent, applicable only to a relative few people. Politicians, present and future, will be eager to expand and increase the scope of the new system, and taxpayers must remain vigilant and hold each debate in earnest accountability to us as taxpayers to keep it simple, fair, and equitable at all times.

Questions linger, such as whether a Fair Tax would inhibit productivity, or spawn underground markets, and just what "necessities" would be excluded. Likewise, what would become of charitable or mortgage interest deductions under a Flat Tax? Each of these merits debate, but they are soluble and not sacred if we consider the solutions outcomes. Considering our current system has the IRS shelling out $50 million for its agents to learn line dancing at sleep-away camp, billions in given away false tax refunds to foreigners, even an imperfect replacement represents a serious improvement. I seriously doubt that anyone will worry about deducting their mortgage expenses and other items if they are no longer oppressed with their tax filing and giving a fair nudge over fifty percent of their income away in total taxes as it is right now. The fairness of this system is that EVERYONE pays the same, including corporations... we have nothing like this now with the exception of our gasoline taxes. The understood tax burden of pay as you go will be greatly appreciated when most consider the past alternatives. If you throw local sales tax in the pile and abolish the local school, fire, police and state and local tax burdens on property it would make this choice even easier for us to make our lives much less stressful with regard to all forms of our government. I much prefer a pay as you go system.

Further to that, while we remember that this discussion was brought about by scandals at the IRS, including hassling of groups seeking tax-exempt status, along with audits and harassment of people who donated to political candidates or raised their voices in the public square, the issue should not be consumed by politics or prosecutions and the continued persecution of millions hurt during 2008-2012 economic financial crisis that have been devastated and now find the IRS being their biggest nemesis for recovering.

Odious as the IRS is, we have allowed this beast to live and survive far too long. When you create an unaccountable, bloated bureaucracy, their benefactors are the sorts of people who show up to run it. They and their ilk are not unique to history, nor are they helpful in solving the problem.

So again, which should we choose, a Fair Tax or a Flat Tax? The answer is: whichever one can gain traction. I prefer the hybrid solution so long as the IRS and income tax goes bye-bye.

The primary question of whether to abolish the IRS having been answered in the affirmative by both sides, disagreement between Fair Tax and Flat Tax proponents is akin to the quarrels of best or better. The applicable lesson here is, having agreed on the big issue, residual differences can be worked out over breakfast and a few coffees.

And so they should be, with the American people as arbiter to make sure we get true reform and clear and better tax code. Politics being the art of the possible, if there is an appetite in the land for a Fair Tax, and political leadership able to make it happen, Flat Tax folks should sign on, perhaps keeping personal lists of I-told-you-so recipients, in case the system falters. Likewise, if the Flat Tax finds a market and effective champions, Fair Taxers should offer support. Better yet the combination of their two efforts would produce an awesome new hybrid and I believe a highly effective new Flat-Fair Tax code.

Whichever option prevails, let us seize this opportunity to reform America's tax system and change the country for the better, while we still have the time to square away our financial obligations fairly and without draconian new taxes and/or further loss of personal economic freedoms.

CHAPTER SIX

High Taxes Hurt Our Economy

In Fiscal Year (FY) 2011, state and local governments in the United States collected $1,338,436,677,000, or $1.3 trillion, in state and local taxes. The list of taxes include property taxes, sales and excise taxes, individual and corporate income taxes, licenses, and severance taxes to name a few. While this is an impressive sum of money, it tells us little about whether or not the average American taxpayer can afford this level of taxation.

In order to compare the burden of tax systems across states, there must be a common yardstick. The most common yardstick is to measure tax collections against the size of the economy as defined by total personal income (which is mostly wages and salaries, interest, dividends, and rent, and personal current transfer receipts [Social Security, Medicare, and Medicaid]). Based on this metric, state and local taxes consumed 10.5 cents our every dollar earned in America, or 10.5 percent of personal income in FY 2011. And the tax burden has grown by a whopping 42.1 percent to 10.5 percent in FY 2011 from 7.4 percent in FY 1950.

Having a clear understanding of the tax burden is

important because taxes matter to the countless number of economic decisions made everyday in our economy. Taxes influence the location of businesses, where people shop, and the wealth of nations. Unfortunately, many taxes are hidden and make it nearly impossible for the average American to understand. The goal of the analysis presented here is to shed light on America's tax burden so that taxpayers and policymakers can make better decisions.

Today the government in all forms, meaning state, local and federal government take approximately a fifty two percent slice of every dollar you earn. This is in the form of licensure, property taxes, sales taxes, income taxes, payroll taxes and excise taxes. Don't you think it is time that we were allowed to keep more of our pay check than all the politicians and their fat cat junkets, lavish lifestyles, and excessive personal benefits that are so out of touch with America they have no comprehension of the average Americans economic plight. They live on sound bytes and polls and use scare tactics to keep American's bamboozled into believing that this huge economic weight around our necks is acceptable and the price of freedom. There is nothing further from the truth. By abolishing our tax code in favor of a new hybrid tax code built on low corporate gross receipts taxes, no personal income taxes, national consumption, excise and licensure and import fees our nation would lead the economic rebirth of the entire global economy.

The United States would once again be the center for all

innovation, economic investment and the greatest magnet of creative and entrepreneurial people in the world. This would be the single greatest and most successful economic development policy of the past one hundred years and this entire century.

CHAPTER SEVEN

Failed Efforts of the Past...

'The third agency of government I would – I would do away with [is] Education, Commerce and, let's see. I can't. The third one, I can't. Sorry. Oops."

I would wager that Texas Governor Rick Perry would give anything to forget that embarrassing memory malfunction during the Republican primary debate leading up to the last election of 2012. For the record the agency Governor Perry couldn't remember was, well, now this is embarrassing. Wait, I got it, the IRS.

What's funny is that Perry was actually talking about his flat tax plan and somehow got sidetracked. In any case, he was definitely onto something, just as President Bush was with his desire to create a national voucher system for workforce benefits.

I'd bet some serious money that everybody and anyone reading this would love to do away with the dreaded IRS. Why else would you be reading this article if you don't believe this to be something most of us would desire? It's so simple, really. Just implement a flat tax system and/or combination flat tax and fair tax, do away with the whole 70,000-page tax code and, voila, no more IRS. Life is good.

Russia's has had great success with its thirteen percent (13%) flat tax rate. Tax revenues are up and so is the economy. And Perry is far from alone in proposing a flat tax in America. Steve Forbes, Jerry Brown (that's right, a Democrat), and Mr. Flat Tax himself, the late great Jack Kemp, all advocated for a flat tax system. Congressional legend Dick Armey also championed it for years while in Congress.

The Original Armey-Shelby Flat Tax proposed

The Armey-Shelby flat tax would replace our progressive federal income tax with a proportional tax of 17 percent. Both individuals and businesses would pay the 17 percent, and no deductions or credits would be allowed. The only income that would not be taxed would be a personal exemption that every taxpayer would receive. For a family of four, no tax would be paid on the first $35,400 of income.

Those in favor of the flat tax believe that it is fairer than the present system because everyone is taxed at the same rate. They stress that the flat tax would be so simple that taxpayers could file their taxes on a postcard-sized form. Proponents also insist that the economy would not only prosper but would grow under the flat tax, although tight spending controls would be placed on the budget.

Supporters believed that the flat tax, although proportional in principle, is progressive in practice. Because of the high family exemption, the more taxpayers earn, the larger the share of income they pay in tax. As illustrated in the chart, a family of four with an income of $25,000 would not pay tax because they are under the $35,400 exemption. A family of four with an income of $50,000 would pay only 6 percent of its earnings because of the exemption; that is, it is paying only on the amount remaining after $35,400 is subtracted from the $50,000. A family of four with an income of $200,000, on the other hand, would pay 14 percent of its earnings under the flat tax.

Fair Tax

A completely different proposal for replacing the existing federal income tax is a national sales tax known as the Fair Tax. Its proponents explain that their Fair Tax is a voluntary "consumption" tax. The idea behind their plan is that the more a person buys, the more tax that individual pays. The less the person buys, the less taxes that person pays.

Although the tax is proportional in principle, supporters see it as progressive in the belief that wealthy people spend more money than people at other income levels do. They would make the tax less regressive to low-income groups by not taxing necessities. All income levels would also receive a (Prebate) rebate based on the number of people in the household. Under the Fair Tax, there would no longer be corporate taxes, business-to-business taxes, self-employment taxes, taxes on investments or savings, or estate and inheritance taxes.

"Over 68% of Americans support a Fair and/or Flat Tax and the abolishment of the IRS tax code or progressive taxation system and converting to a Fair or Flat Tax code."

According to Debate.org (2)

The Rebirth of the American Dream

CHAPTER EIGHT

The IRS must be Minimized to a Regulatory Role!

Now that the IRS has been caught more or less red-handed targeting Tea Party members and other conservative opponents of President Obama prior to the 2012 presidential election, I can't think of a better time to do away with the one government agency that is so hopelessly broken every American knows it can't be fixed and that every American hates with the same passion.

Don't even get me started on the agency's new charter to manage the implementation and enforcement of ObamaCare, provide home loans and even settle past due taxes without haggling. I just checked their website link to the settlement page and just like the Obamacare website the link was broken and not working. Come on, this is the greatest most sophisticated technology country in the world, how does our massive government put up such offers and then hide behind the oops... website is down excuse? The federal government having access to our medical data is scary enough; the idea that the IRS is in charge of that is downright terrifying, especially when you see the penalties that they will be allowed to apply and enforce without any real oversight or accountability. Many of the current estimates demonstrate that the cost of Obamacare for a family of four will top $20,000 per year. How is that affordable? But if it is mandatory and we can't afford it, we will be indebt to the IRS and they will hound us into our graves for the money... they will get it and at what cost to all of us? Ask yourself, do you really want the IRS in our medical care discussion? They already terrify most people and for good reason, they are abusive and non-responsive to the taxpayer's actual situation and abilities to pay.

Let's look at the alternative and what's good for small business America is good for all Americans. Here are some of the benefits from a flat tax system and the abolishment of the IRS overhaul and elimination.

Everybody will pay income tax. Today, nearly half of all Americans pay no income tax. That means they have no skin in the game. Under a flat tax, if you make very little you pay very little; if you make a lot you pay a lot. The concept that those who make more should pay a higher tax rate is fatally flawed. It actually penalizes people for being successful. Those who make more do pay more even in the scenario of a combination flat and fair tax... everyone spends money.

It will simplify everyone's life. No more 70,000-page tax code. No more Alternative Minimum Tax (AMT) or any other idiotic schemes, for that matter. No more tax year-end mad scramble. No more having to keep all sorts of crazy records. Simple is best and collecting at the point of sale is preferred.

There's bipartisan support. While it's true that flat tax supporters have mostly been Republicans, during the 2012 election campaign, everyone, even President Obama, said they thought the tax code needed to be overhauled, they just didn't want to offer any real solutions. This is something we can all get behind, for once. In fact, a savvy and smart Presidential candidate would endorse this approach, and it would propel them to a huge victory in the next election.

We'd all save money on day one. Whether you're an individual, a small business, or a big corporation, whatever you spend to do your taxes, you'll save it right off the bat. I just have a one-person company and a family of four and it costs thousands to do our taxes every year. Reclaiming that would go straight to the bottom line and get spent in the economy and that would have an exponential indirect and direct economic impact on local economies.

No more corporate loopholes, and less lobbying. Corporations lobby Washington to impact three things: regulations, laws, and tax rules. A flat tax with no deductions will eliminate the latter. Every company will pay their own flat corporate revenue tax so it is fair to every company.

It will cut up to $10 billion or more a year off the federal budget. In all seriousness, I don't think we can or need to actually unravel the entire agency, just defang it and have it focus on accounting for the point of sale receipts and corporate taxes on revenues from the published sales reports, but if we go the flat and fair tax route, we should be able to cut at least eight $8 or nine $9 billion out of the federal budget. Yes, there will still need to be accountants and CPAs.

It will increase our tax revenues. If you buy into the ***Laffer Curve*** as so many economists do, then you believe there's an optimum tax rate for maximizing tax income. That's what happened in Russia and, if we do it right, it will happen here. It will also help us balance the budget and reduce our ballooning debt.

The Theoretical Economic Concept of Supply Side Economics and the impact of taxation on positive economic growth are theorized to work like this.

"The Laffer Curve is one of the main theoretical constructs of supply-side economics, and is often used as a shorthand to sum up the entire pro-growth world view of supply-side economics. However, the Laffer Curve itself simply illustrates the tradeoff between tax rates and the total tax revenues actually collected by the government.

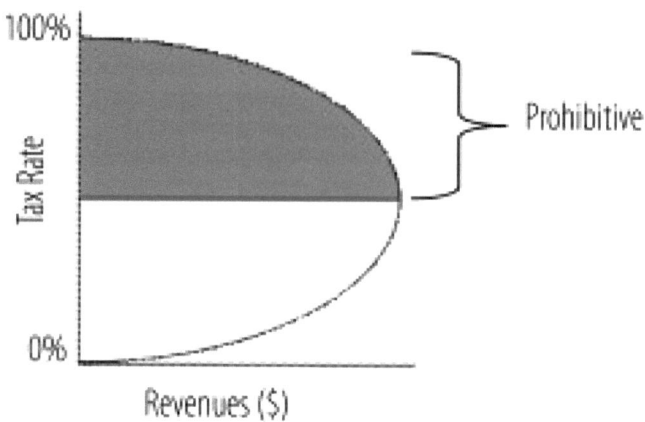

As drawn, the Laffer-Curve shows that at a tax rate of 0%, the government would collect no tax revenue, just as it would collect no tax revenue at a tax rate of 100% because no one would be willing to work for an after-tax wage of zero. The reason for this is that tax rates have two effects on revenues: one is arithmetic, the other economic." (3)

What is important is to note that the Laffer-Curve does not say whether a tax cut will raise or lower revenues outright, nor does it predict that any and all tax rate reductions would necessarily bring in more total revenues. The concept of the economic stimulus is simple it is based on Economic Impact models such as Direct Economic Impact, those revenues and economic gains such as jobs, discretionary spending from surplus, and Indirect Economic Impact, those gains created due to the additional weight of such expenditures on all the industries that realize a benefit from the new spending, so additional jobs created and economic outcomes from the new influx of economic growth.

What the curve does say is that tax rate reductions will always result in a smaller loss in revenues than one would have expected when relying only on the static estimates of the previous tax base. This also means that the higher the starting tax rate, the more dramatic the supply-side stimulus will be from cutting the tax rate. This is somewhat obvious if you are stymied by oppressive payments to the government and now you have some relief, people begin to live and spend more freely on themselves, which has far more benefits on the economy than an induced benefit of paying our governments and allowing them to dole out the good will of their own version of economics. It is possible that this economic effect will swamp the arithmetic effect, causing an actual increase in tax revenue.

However, the Laffer-Curve does not say, "all tax cuts pay for themselves" as many people have claimed, they are exaggerating to impress people and their audience. I do not believe we have to stretch the truth; the truth is clear cut without such follies. What is true is that tax rate cuts will always lead to more growth, employment, and income for citizens, which are desirable outcomes leading to greater prosperity and opportunity in the whole of our society. There is, after all, more to fiscal policy than simply maximizing government revenue.

It's all-good as long as we act. So to summarize the Laffer-Curve predicted impact of lowering our taxes, we get More jobs, More disposable income and More opportunities for innovation and the restoration of the American Dream.

This should be advocated for any person, organization or institution that believes that economic development is at its' core the creation of an environment where opportunity can flourish and become globally competitive and by doing so reward those in the locale by growing their economic opportunities through wages, enhanced recreational and lifestyle affordability and new affordable services for their use and welfare.

It will boost our sluggish economy. This is the argument for doing it now. We need it now to boost our sluggish economy but we'll need it going forward to improve our competitiveness in global markets. Our current economy has been flat and volatile and to say the least extremely fragile. And favorable corporate tax rates will incentivize companies to repatriate capital to our shores and create new investment and jobs here. The abolishment of the current IRS tax code would be the greatest economic development tool introduced by our governments and for once it would be fair across the board in all fifty states.

We could all sleep better at night. The only people that won't sleep better at night are the IRS employees and independent tax accountants that will be affected. Indeed, they will have to be retrained and redeployed but that should only be temporary and it is no different than the tens of millions of other Americans that have had to do the same thing for their own occupations and careers having to face the persistent and ever ongoing changes of the global economy. With all that extra money floating around, we'll need even more bean counters, more talented people than ever. Job growth should double within the first eighteen months.

Look, this is a simple equation: If we implement a flat and fair tax system and get rid of most of the IRS we bring in more tax revenue, boost the economy, reduce the federal deficit and national debt, and benefit every individual and business, big and small. That's all there is to it. This is not nearly as difficult as the media and those in power want the average American citizen to be led to believe. It simply requires a unified grassroots effort that is relentless in our pursuit of life, liberty and the pursuit of happiness!

CHAPTER NINE

What would the New Hybrid Tax Code Be?

So we have heard the arguments against the oppressive progressive tax system we have now and its' abusive enforcer the Internal Revenue Service, so let's look at what the new tax code might look like and why it will work for everyone in the United States, and most of all be fair, impartial and equitable to all of us living, working and recreating within our borders.

First you must divide our tax responsibility as a nation into two distinct categories, the corporate taxes and the personal taxes. Then you must take those down to the various governmental jurisdictional levels. A tax code according to our US Constitution has to be fair and equitable across the board. Therefore jockeying with the tax code was not something that our fore fathers and founding fathers felt was in the best interest of Americans.

Corporate Taxation

I am in favor of a straight forward and simple to understand and therefore simple to enforce tax code at all levels of government and across the board whether corporate or personal.

I do not believe that imposing massive taxes on corporations is the correct economic development systemic method to grow our national or other state and local economies. This has created an entire industry of incentives being doled out by governments at the state and local level to attract new investments by corporations, retain existing companies and grow their job basis. This has taken a heavy amount of criticism in the media and at local governmental public hearings when such incentives are being ratified and awarded to various companies based on promised outcomes of new investment and jobs normally. I have always advocated that under our current tax code this is not only appropriate but also realistic and that criticism of such tactics is naïve. But, if we moved to a new tax code that is flat and fair, this type of business investment incentives use would not be a major component of new investment decisions by companies. In fact, as I have stated earlier a new flat corporate tax that is modest would probably result in a huge influx of new company investments to inshore their operations to the United States, in order to avoid other countries oppressive taxation.

So what would the most likely fair and flat tax be for corporations you might ask?

It would depend is the answer. There is not a one tax does it all approach. You have to account for excise taxes, import taxes (tariffs) and income taxes. These are the big three that I believe merit the most discussion and can cover the lion share of our central governments revenue needs for what we should expect of their role in our own lives.

Let's just agree on what most Americans' believe that role is by definition. First and foremost is to keep us safe from harm by outside influences such as foreign nations acting aggressively against the United States people and terrorism, so the military and intelligence infrastructure. Second is the promotion of trade, commerce and diplomacy globally and the representation of our fair treatment as traders and travelers abroad. Lastly, it is the governments provision to protect our innate rights granted by the US constitution, the pursuit of life, liberty and happiness, while maintaining our general welfare as a people. I group this into regulatory oversight of what we have access to and how we are assured it will work properly and not allow us to be harmed by anything that is not legitimate in our pursuit of these dreams. Regulatory can become quite large as it must view our finances, education, energy, utilities infrastructure, healthcare, travel and workforce benefits to name a few.

So I know I have simplified this matter a good bit. I did this simplification because at the root issue of most of these central core government roles (regulatory, military and diplomacy) the costs can be covered by the three forms of taxation I discussed without income tax. I agree with the general use of these other forms of taxation if they are done fairly and flat across the board, and are not done with additional income to support these efforts. It is my straight forward belief that our pay as you go cost of governing and paying off our current national debt needs to be done so out of existing cash flow, not borrowed future obligations, that we have no realistic expectation we can afford to repay. Doing our current system is just another huge financial calamity in the making and we all know this to be true, so we can't continue or allow our nation to continue down this ruinous path.

Excise (Use) Taxes- Perhaps the most invisible taxes for most consumers are these taxes on items that we use that the government can use to target specific funding needs. The best example is gasoline tax at the pumps. Those taxes are then doled out to improve roads, rebuild bridges and create better transportation arteries for traffic flow and relief of congestion. They can also fund alternative transportation such as trains, light rail, and bus transportation. Excise taxes can cover a broad host of our needs and thus can be utilized for many of our basic services such as telecommunications, water, sewer, electricity, gas and even clean energy production. Portions of the excise taxes can be allocated to improve and create better delivery of all these products. The fuel tax could be expanded to provide a small incentive to those companies and individuals that choose to invest in highly efficient vehicle, the gas and electricity tax can be used to fund energy efficiency through credits to those that improve the energy efficiency of their facilities and homes. In my book, the Next America, I discuss that our biggest energy savings would come from using such incentives to improve our vehicle efficiency and home and facilities energy efficiency.

Another example of how to better use Excise taxes is best understood by looking at the entire concept of our monetary system and the Federal Reserve Board's control of our funds cost to borrow. There is of course the Federal Insurance on Deposits that could be covered through small transaction taxes on Ecommerce of say, ½ one half of a percent up to some cap rate of say a $30.00 for major purchases and/or wire payments. Banks charge fees now for receiving and sending such payments. The federal government could set those funds aside to provide for regulatory compliance of our money systems and cover depositors up to the insured amount, so no more bailouts would be required from the taxpayers, it would be a self-funded system.

The same concept can be applied to cigarettes, alcohol and tobacco products to provide for addictive behaviors and the cost of treatment and research on disease cures for medicine. The use of excise taxes would allow us to target our needs with a funding source aside from our own everyone legally paying taxes today pays system. Non-smokers, non-drinkers and such would not be penalized with the burden of these costs, which seems fair to me.

Tariff (Import) Taxes- This is a very sticky subject because we have agreements such as GAT (General Agreement on Trade) and the WTO (World Trade Organization) that we need to be mindful of. But essentially, we need to provide for adequate homeland security and inspection of all one hundred percent (100%) of goods shipped into this country. This will require a massive increase in such inspections, which are abysmal at this point. The cost of such inspections should be passed along to the exporter that is importing to our country and paid in advance. The over-all cost will be borne by the consumer, but many of these items may then become highly price sensitive and many companies may decide that building a facility to produce those goods within the United States is a much better choice that shipping them, especially when you consider the ever increasing cost of energy to get them to market. That would be a real boon for economic development in the United States as a windfall to this activity. There will still be folks that want certain items made in their foreign market, such as Swiss Watches, German automobiles to name a few. Much of our regulatory and compliance on homeland security would then be covered by the activity, so the cost is borne by those consuming the products, as I feel it should be. Choice of avoidance legally is never a bad option in any purchase or tax.

Income (revenue) Taxes- Currently corporations must pay taxes on profits and they play all kinds of games to avoid paying their taxes, which can exceed thirty percent (30%). They are taxed on net profits not their gross. Anyone who is ever in a deal about getting paid on net versus gross already knows the smart bet is on the gross funds taken in. Just look at the movie industry. People, who take a percentage of the net pie, hardly ever see any monies as the expert are awesome at making every production lose money on paper. Well so are companies just as good at this hocus pocus game of hiding profits or reinvesting them into new activities. The argument against my proposal, which is a simple small gross receipts tax, is that somehow companies will choose not to then reinvest in new technologies, discoveries, science, etc. That is hogwash and we all know that. They will reinvest to stay ahead in the game of competition or they will be supplanted by a new company that has done so, it is that simple, compete or be killed by the competition. It's called capitalism. The use of a gross receipts tax of approximately three percent would be a good starting point. It is not enough to hurt any company and it would reduce their cost of tax avoidance. It would also create a ground swell of new investment into the United States, as we would be one of the lowest corporate taxes in the world. So, what would that mean to us as Americans? Oh come on, more jobs! This is why I have argued for the past decade that economic development needs to advocate for this modification in the tax code, it will create a renaissance era in the United States in new economic development across the country.

Personal Taxation- We of course bear the brunt of all taxes as most are passed through to us in the form of the cost of goods and services. The biggest and most offensive abuse of our earned monies is our requirement to simply hand it over to our alleged benevolent government, which has our best interest at heart in their uses. The government has turned into a big time out of control spender that has proven they cannot be trusted with our monies without specific use requirements. Just recall, eight hundred dollar hammers and bridges to nowhere to refresh your memory on this point. Or their alleged having enough surplus monies to cover social security through out our lives. These are just pork barrel politics and unmet promises that could never be fulfilled and they knew they would not be fulfilled. The payroll deductions and federal income taxes are not sufficient to pay for actual unemployment of anyone earning anything above poverty and the same is true of disability and retirement funds as well as the medical provisions they are now proposing. They are not sufficient to balance our budget or pay for the actual cost of operating our central government. Yet, these funds consume upwards of approximately half our earnings. So obviously we will need to trim the federal appetite to fund everything under the sun and focus on what we as American's can actually afford and are willing to pay for... it's our choice, not theirs.

Now we shift to our own personal tax burden as citizens. Let's look at this from the same simple approach. First you must understand that most of the corporate taxes will be absorbed by all of us when we purchase and/or use their products, so they are also paid by us as a people, but they are kept in balance by the sheer nature of competition for our monies between companies. This is the basic concept of capitalism that competition will breed competitive and affordable pricing for such goods and services. In other words, the consumers for the better values will bypass those companies that are not competitive, in the market, because we as consumers always seek the best value. This is the basic concept of capitalism, those that are strong and innovative survive and thrive and those that don't die.

Two forms of taxation can cover all local-State Taxation- the cost of education, fire, police and infrastructure, and local governance. First a state and local portion of the national sales tax. This would be capped at seven percent, so that the over-all national sales tax would not exceed thirty percent across the nation. The additional costs of governance would be covered in our cost of services through excise taxes. Again, this makes us absorb the actual cost of our services in today's costs. It also does not allow us to be held hostage on our hard earned assets such as homes and property. This will require that local government be prudent on their use of taxes and be very cost-conscious, just as we as consumers have to be ourselves. There can be a special sales tax provision passed for specific targeted items such as new recreational facilities, performing and visual arts centers, new recreational amenities, libraries and sports facilities on an individual voter referendum basis if a locale so desires. Much of this can be covered in special ticket taxes and tourism taxes as well (an excise tax again on a specific use). The elimination of property tax will provide for clear full deeded ownership of property without being co-owners with our government. I just think it is wrong that they can sell our assets even when we have paid them off for their own purposes if we do not pay our taxes, that is, just conversion and extortion plain and simple. Fee simple Titled land that is free and clear of the cost of improvements and ownership should be just that, paid for in full.

Federal Taxation- First let me make this clear. I am not in favor of gift taxes, inheritance and/or taxes on dividends and profits and/or the increased value of our homes when they are sold. If the government wants to charge a title tax for transference (a transaction tax or more akin to the old stamp tax of King George two hundred plus years ago) then so be it, but it should be modest and not exceed a few hundred dollars at most, depending on the value of the transaction. We do not owe our profits from monies we have already paid taxes on to the government, which is double taxation straight-forward.

The REAL NEW DEAL...

The new federal taxes would be excise taxes and transaction and use taxes, a national sales tax preferably with a workforce voucher system for private self-directed purchase of our workforce benefits, this tax should not exceed twenty percent. This places our total tax burden per citizen, visitor and illegal alien at less than thirty percent (30%) of our monies spent. Savings would not be taxed ever. The final federal tax would be the tariffs on imports for homeland security and inspection. To me this system would be simple and fair. It will place the government in the proper role of regulatory oversight and compliance on items we use, purchase and depend upon for our welfare and the pursuit of happiness. It does not put them into the business of being our provider of our needs; this price of responsibility comes with each of us as citizens to learn to look out for our own best interests and that of our family. This system is fair and dignified as it places and restores individual responsibility in place of Big Government knowing what is best for us and then acting in their own best interests not our own. We have witnessed this over and over again, so it is time to say enough and stand up against this continued abuse.

What We Have Always Wanted from our Government… is the **_Net Result_** or outcome of this sweeping tax code change. Will be, a clean efficient, fair and equitable tax code that requires very little oversight by the IRS and the government and reduces our personal and corporate stress. It will create a robust instantaneous revenue stream for the provision of our needs as things are purchased and used. The pay as you go system is highly more efficient and increases cash flow, which in turn requires we increase our scrutiny of how the government will use these increased revenue streams. The reason I know it will increase is simple, today nearly fifty percent of people are net benefactors to the tax code, meaning they take more than they pay. With this system everyone will contribute their fair share including visitors, aliens and citizens. The black market or underground economy or what some call the invisible economy has been estimated to be approximately fifteen percent (15%) of our actual economy, estimated at over two trillion dollars, $2 trillion today. (6) This alone will create a huge revenue boon, but it will be fair to all folks in the United States.

CHAPTER TEN

Final thoughts

Most of us as Americans have been taught to play by the rules and that the rules have been established to protect us from unfair treatment, tyranny and abusive powers by unauthorized folks and to generally keep the peace and promote the general welfare of everyone. So, it should not surprise any of us that we are tired and fed up with one major agency being able to totally ignore such concepts in their dealings with us as citizens. Our bloated central government has become so out of touch with most of our own stresses that they just want to maintain their status quo and keep their lucrative and luxurious lifestyle. Their pit bull strong arm agents at the IRS are becoming more and more powerful, all the while we as citizens are losing individual freedoms, economic security and our sanity and much worse the belief in the American Dream is fading very quickly especially for the baby boomers that lost the most during the most recent economic recession.

It has to be our nations will and effort to restore the greatness to our nation at its' core values of fairness, equality and opportunity for all that come and want to work hard and create new innovations and economic expansion both through individual new wealth and community wealth growth. We all know the current system is neither fair nor equitable across the board. The fixes as I have discussed are not draconian, they are not unfathomable economic theories, they are not oppressive to anyone individual, any income bracket, to any minority or any persons in general, and they are reasonable and sound. The continued stalling of enacting these solutions is only creating more economic harm to all of us now, and future generations.

It is a very famous quote that comes to mind in this discussion of what many refer to as radical changes to our American tax code and our over-all fiscal responsibility, "You are either part of the solution or part of the problem, which are you, you cannot ride the fence on this issue?" If we all continue to allow our nation to be eroded and our core values to be destroyed and our fiscal mindset to be even more jaded away from capitalism in favor of other forms of less free societies then we will inherit for our future generations a very different America than our founding fathers envisioned so long ago. We must all be accountable for taking action and voicing our strong belief in what needs to be done to get our nation back on a sound economic footing and create a fair economic opportunity for all of us that choose and desire to live, work and recreate here. There have been far too many Americans hurt by our current lack of a good tax code, lack of fiscal responsibility and lack of our economic recovery. CNN estimated in 2012 that there are over eight six million (86) American workers that are invisible and no longer eligible for unemployment and/or have given up on dignified reemployment. (5) Fair is not difficult and it is not unfair, it is simply easy and direct. Take your own initiative and write and call your elected officials and voice your concerns over our local, state and federal tax policies. Changing these policies will do more to resurrect the American Dream than anything else we as a people can do right now!

God Bless America! The Land of Free People with a voice for what is right and an eye for fairness in all matters. Stand up and be accountable it is the cost of being a good citizen... you owe this to yourself and our future generations.

The End

Don Allen Holbrook

FOOTNOTE REFERENCES;

1.) Sauter, Michael, USA Today, October 28, 2012- "States with the Highest Income Taxes"

2.) Debate.org "American's Favor a Fair or Flat Tax" Dec 3, 2013

http://www.debate.org/opinions/is-a-flat-tax-system-better-than-a-progressive-tax

3.) The Laffer-Center, Dec 4, 2013

http://www.laffercenter.com/the-laffer-center-2/the-laffer-curve/

4.) Taxation History of United States

http://en.wikipedia.org/wiki/Taxation_history_of_the_United_States

5.) Censky, Annalyn, CNN, America's Job Crisis, "The 86 Million Invisible Unemployed" May 12, 2012

http://money.cnn.com/2012/05/03/news/economy/unemployment-rate/

6.) Staff Report, The Daily Bell, "2 Trillion Underground Economy" April 26, 2013

http://www.thedailybell.com/news-analysis/29040/2-Trillion-US-Underground-Economy-Is-the-Free-Market-Striking-Back/

Don Allen Holbrook

ABOUT THE AUTHOR

Don Holbrook is a private consultant involved in economic development public policy, site location decisions for private sector investments by companies for new facilities that create jobs and attract local investment to communities. He is one of the few practitioner-based economists in the field of economic development. His non-fiction books on local economic development efforts to rebuild, renew and regain sustainably balanced economic development public policy that will lead to creating world-class communities has been a groundbreaking successes within his industry. His first book, the "Little Black Book of Economic Development" has spawned a series of follow-up books on how communities, companies, individuals and families can navigate these treacherous economic times to achieve their economic goals.

Holbrook is one of the worlds foremost thought leaders and public speakers on the subject of how communities can build smart and sustainable local grassroots driven economic development strategies to achieve maximum success in what he refers to as "The Art of the Deal Today."

Holbrook is a Certified Economic Developer and in 2008 he was formally indoctrinated as a Fellow Member of the International Economic Development Council, for his lifetime achievements by his peers.

He lives with wife and two sons in Las Vegas, Nevada.

Holbrook during his world travels became fascinated with the medieval historical period surrounding the Poor Fellow Soldiers of Christ of the Temple of Solomon, more commonly known today as the Knights Templars. He has written two fictional books on this subject. In 2010, Holbrook was formally knighted at West Point USMA as a member of the modern day Sovereign Military Order of the Temple of Jerusalem, the Knights Templar Order.

Don Allen Holbrook

www.ingramcontent.com/pod-product-compliance
Lightning Source LLC
Chambersburg PA
CBHW040905180526
45159CB00010BA/2935